THE JOURNEY TO
BEAUTIFUL LIVING

SEVEN PILLARS FOR LIVING A
FULFILLED LIFE

———————

Keisa L. Campbell

THE JOURNEY TO BEAUTIFUL LIVING
Copyright © 2024 by Keisa L. Campbell

ISBN: 979-8-9900486-0-7
ISBN: 979-8-9900486-1-4 (hardcover)
ISBN: 979-8-9900486-2-1 (ebook)

Printed in the USA

DEDICATION

To every woman, my heartfelt prayer is that you never lose sight of your true essence and that you continuously strive to embrace life to its fullest.

TABLE OF CONTENTS

INTRODUCTION

A journey to living a fulfilled life is what I call Beautiful Living. I believe that we all desire to live a life of joy and fulfillment but we often neglect to seek it out. We live in the rat race of life until one day we look up and realize that time has passed us by. Then we wonder what we have done with our lives and sometimes we find ourselves lost and void of clear directions to move forward.

Society has trained us to look at external situations for temporary fulfillment. If we are not careful, we will find ourselves constantly chasing what was never meant to bring permanent fulfillment; careers, relationships, material things. Instead, take some time and look inward. Envision the things that you want out of life and don't you dare think for a second that you are too old to do what God has placed in your heart. Every day above ground is an opportunity that you get to do what He is calling you to do.

There are several accounts of my life's story that I will share throughout this book that I hope will inspire you to look at your life and take your own action to live a beautiful life. You only have one life. I know that's cliché, but it's true. So, what will you do with the remaining time that you have left? It's time to take an audit of your life so that you can move to where you want to be.

ONE

How the Journey Began

"Trust in the LORD with all your heart and lean not on your

own understanding; in all your ways submit to him, and he will

make your paths straight."

Proverbs 3:5-6 (NIV)

Life, though beautiful, can be very challenging at times. The challenge of life began for me at 14 years of age when I gave birth to my beautiful daughter. I quickly realized that I didn't want to be a statistic and that my life wasn't about me anymore.

I made it my number one priority to graduate from high school with my graduating class because every decision that I made from that point on would impact my baby girl as well.

Should I go away to college, or to attend a local college? Should I work a full-time job, or should I go to school full-time? Should I work full-time and go to school part-time, or should I fulfill my mother's desire for me to go into the Airforce? I knew I didn't want to join the military, so I needed to make a decision that would positively impact my life as well as my daughter's.

The first vision that I had for my life came to pass. Not only did I finish high school on time with my graduating class, but I also received the HOPE scholarship to attend college. I didn't apply for college during my senior year because I wasn't sure what I wanted to major in and no one around me encouraged me to go to college. Since I was a teen mom, I didn't even have the support of my high school counselor to aid me in the process. It was all on me. My friends were going off to college and I decided that I would further my education as well, but I needed to figure out what that looked like for me.

Since I accomplished my first goal of finishing high school with my class, the next thing I had to figure out was what I wanted my life to look like as a young mom and adult. Who did I want to become and what was it going to take to become her? Either way, I knew that I needed to work.

I started working at a local public school system in high school and continued working there. As a result, I decided that I would begin by attending a two-year institution and go to school in the evenings. My major was undeclared at the time, but I knew I wanted to help people. After a semester I decided to go to school for Nursing.

I knew I was on to something because Nursing would directly help others. I continued school in the evenings, excited about the opportunity to impact the lives of others by becoming a nurse. All was good until one day, my mom, my sister, and aunt were in a bad car accident, leaving my aunt with a cracked pelvic bone and my sister with a broken ankle and toe. She had to have screws put in and when she came home, she needed someone to change the gauze and bandages.

My mom would suggest that since I was in school for nursing, I could do it. I couldn't bring myself to it. Everything inside me cringed. The dream of being a nurse was short-lived and the next school day, I went and withdrew from the program. Nursing wasn't my calling and I'm glad that I realized it sooner than later.

In high school, I thought that I would advance my education by becoming a licensed hairstylist, but I quickly dismissed this idea because of the negativity that surrounded me when it came to my desire to do hair. My boyfriend, who would later become my husband, asked me what I wanted to do with my life, and my response was to do hair.

He replied, "Is that what you want to do with your life, be a hairstylist? I know you can think of something else besides that." That statement made me feel as if being a hairstylist was mediocre and that I should explore other things. I knew that doing hair was a gift and talent, but his words haunted me so much so that when people would ask me who did my hair, I would cringe and reply, "Me" because I knew the next question would be "Oh, you do hair? Can you do mine? Are you in a shop?" (By the way ladies, it's a salon. You take your car to the shop.)

Since I felt like styling hair wasn't good enough, I in turn didn't feel that I was good enough to do theirs. Later in life, I spoke to my husband about how his statement made me feel and he apologized stating that he didn't know any better at the time. He said that knowing what he knew in the present moment, his response would have been different. His initial statement stayed with me for many years even beyond bringing it to his attention.

While trying to figure out my career choice, I continued to work at the local public school system. I also began doing hair out of my house here and there despite the comment that was made to me and I was in love and pregnant with my second daughter. At this point in my life, I was about to get married. I turned twenty-one years old and gave birth to my second daughter seven days after my birthday. My wedding was just four months away and I still hadn't finished college.

As a wife and a mother of two, it was still my desire to finish college. So, I decided to enroll in cosmetology school. What I knew was, people were asking me to do their hair often and I was good at it, so I went for it. I stayed the course and was on track to earn my cosmetology diploma. I made straight A's while earning my diploma and was recognized in the National Technical Honor

Society (NTHS). I passed the state board practical exam on the first try, which doesn't happen for many. I became a licensed cosmetologist! The very thing that I was discouraged from becoming was the very thing that helped us survive some rough financial patches in my marriage.

At this point in my life, when considering what I wanted my life to look like and who I wanted to become, the things I knew for sure were: I wanted to own my own business, I was good at doing hair, I wanted to help others, and I wanted to earn my college degree.

When I was a few months shy of twenty-seven, I had my third daughter and being a wife and mother took precedence in my life. I wanted to be the best mom and wife that I could be, but I still hadn't accomplished my dreams of obtaining my college degree. Yes, I had graduated with honors from my cosmetology program, however, it was still my desire to obtain a bachelor's degree. I took classes here and there, at this school and at that school, all while ensuring that the desires of my husband's and children's hearts came to pass.

It was my heart's desire to become a psychologist, but I realized that the traditional four-year semester state colleges weren't going to help me reach my goal and that it would be years before I would be able to finish. I was only able to take a certain number of classes and they were all semester-based so I transferred to a private college that did not have psychology as a major. I knew I wanted my own business/practice, so I switched my major to business. Taking mini-mesters and moving at an accelerated pace was what I needed.

In-between making my family dreams come true, and with my husband's help, I managed to graduate number one in my class, Summa Cum Laude, and was the banner carrier for my field of study with my Associate's Degree in Business Administration. This happened five years after giving birth to my last daughter. One year later, I graduated Summa Cum Laude with my Bachelor's Degree in Business Administration.

I had now accomplished my second vision and goal that I had for myself with three busy children and a husband. No, it wasn't the traditional four years and out track for me, life happened as it does for everyone, but I never lost sight of what I desired in my heart. I kept going despite how it looked. I rewrote the plan, but not the vision or the goal.

Based on your current situation, many of you have given up on those things that your heart once longed for because of what it looks like. It's your own race, not anyone else's. Don't change the vision or the goal, change the route that you will take to get there.

Although I earned my cosmetologist diploma, my associate's, and my bachelor's degree, I still wasn't sure what I was supposed to be doing with my life. I eventually stop doing hair in my house and began working in a hair salon part-time along with my full-time job at the local school system. It appeared that I was good at making others' dreams come true and would be extremely happy about that but was struggling to realize what it was that brought me fulfillment. I was overlooking it.

I would often call family meetings and ask my family what they wanted to do at that moment with their lives. The girls would say, "Cheer or dance" and I would say, "done." I knew it was my husband's desire to be a full-time actor and knowing the dynamics of his job and the difficulty around being able to make an audition because of his 9 to 5, I told him to quit his job and pursue his acting career. I said this without looking at finances or questioning whether I would be able to sustain our family by myself (more about this in Chapter Seven) but no one asked me what it was that I wanted. I always knew that I was to help others, but the "how" I didn't know.

I continued to work both jobs. I knew that the full-time job at the local school system wasn't what I was being called to do, but it was what paid the bills and allowed my family to operate as it did at the time. It also afforded me the opportunity to pop into my children's schools to sit in class and have lunch with them. I couldn't walk away from the hair salon because I knew that was directly impacting the lives of the women who sat in my chair. We became family, I became their therapist, makeup artist, and stylist all from behind the chair. And it was also extra income that provided a cushion for the household.

A few years later, I found myself chasing other things in an effort to find my purpose. I found myself working at the local school system, working part-time in the hair salon, mentoring at-risk juvenile boys, and running a multi-level marketing (MLM) business with a team, volunteering in the hair salon at my church all while being a full-time dance mom to a daughter that danced competitively and had to be at practice six days a week. I did all of this at the same time plus much more.

Although the things that I was doing were directly impacting the lives of others, I still did not feel completely fulfilled. I knew I was to serve others but the "how" and "who" was still a mystery. I had been serving children, women, and MLM teams, by mentoring, training, styling, and coaching from behind the chair, not realizing that's what I was doing. I became burned out.

One night, I cried out to God and I told Him that I couldn't go another day without knowing what I was supposed to be doing with my life. With a snotty nose and while lying in the fetal position, I pleaded with Him to show me so that I could start moving in that direction. I cried myself to sleep. I wanted to know, I desperately had to know, and I was trusting that God heard my cry.

The next morning, God had an answer for me. I heard this still small voice say to me, "Life coaching." I responded, "Life coaching?" I heard the still small voice again say, "Life coaching." I repeated, "Life coaching?" For I had never heard of life coaching before, but I was so thrilled that God heard my cry and jumped up. I was eager, eager to find out what life coaching was so that I can begin to move in the direction of life coaching.

I ran to the computer and pulled up my best friend, Google and I googled life coaching. To my surprise, there was such a thing called life coaching. It wasn't a new thing, but it was something that I had never heard of before. I always had a desire to be a psychologist because I felt like that was the way to help people to get better and live better lives. Since the college that I had transferred to didn't have psychology, I thought life coaching was the next best thing that I could do, and I was overly excited for the opportunity to get started as a certified professional life coach.

I found a life coaching school that I was interested in attending to become a certified professional life coach and they were offering the opportunity to sit in a class before registering to experience and learn more about becoming a coach. I was like YES, sign me up! During the overview, the instructor asked for two volunteers, and I was so utterly excited that God had told me that life coaching was my path, that I volunteered. She needed one to be the life coach and she needed another person to be the client. She chose me to be the life coach.

After learning that I would be the life coach in this sample, I was nervous. I didn't know the first thing about being a life coach, I just learned about what a life coach was just a day or so prior to class but I said, "I can do this. I got this." The instructor asked the other volunteer to be the client and to present a real-life scenario to me. She did and I didn't know how to respond in "life coach" fashion, so every time I responded the instructor was harsh to me saying, "Are you not listening? That was not a good follow-up question," and more negative things.

When the exercise was over, I wanted to hang it up. I felt embarrassed, not good enough, and I instantly thought God told me the wrong thing. I was like lady, that's why I'm here to learn but I didn't say it out my mouth. Quickly the idea of becoming a life coach was no longer. I decided that I was not going to be a life coach, that I wasn't good enough and that God had given me the wrong direction.

While still trying to figure out what my true purpose was, I knocked my hormones completely out of whack. This was one way for God to get my attention. Mentoring, building a multi-level marketing (MLM) team, being a full-time dance mom, volunteering at the hair salon at my church, and working a full-time and part-time job, all earned me the "Superwoman" cape by my friends. I was doing too much, juggling numerous responsibilities without giving myself a moment to breathe or reflect. This relentless pace eventually took a toll on my health, forcing my body to intervene.

I was forced to hang up my cape and clear my plate of the many things that had been consuming my time and energy (more about this in Chapter Four). After experiencing knocking my hormones out of balance, I had no desire to resume any of those previous commitments but nonetheless, I still desired to pursue my purpose.

I remember getting out of my car one day and as I was approaching the steps to my house, I heard God say to me again, "Life coaching." I paused to take in what I heard and decided that I would give it another shot. I went back to researching schools and came across this foundation just for coaching and found a school that was listed.

I reached out to them and enrolled. When asked to be the life coach in class, I happily said yes, and I coached a therapist in a real-life situation and brought her to her aha moment. She cried and thanked me because she had been stuck and she said that coaching with me during that session brought her clarity and direction to what her next steps were supposed to be.

At that moment, I knew what God had spoken to me just a year or two before was true and that I was equipped and worthy and could do what He was calling me to do. Have you ever questioned God after He revealed something to you, and it didn't look like how you thought it should look? Things may not always be straight and narrow. You may experience some twists and turns and some deep curves called life detours, but if you keep seeking, you will see what God has said.

I finally was clear on what I was being called to do; teach, encourage, inspire, motivate, and impact women to live and operate in their purpose so that they can live fulfilling lives.

I continued working at the local school system while curating vision experiences for women to come and get their whole life together (oh there were a few males in attendance). Standing in front of those women, guiding them, and using my expertise brought me so much joy. I had been curating vision experiences when I called meetings with my family in our living room. I had been coaching, inspiring from behind the chair, and teaching while building my MLM team. Even mentoring the juvenile boys and cheering on my girls as they competed and cheered and danced on the sidelines was purposeful. Nothing was wasted.

I started investing in myself, seeking coaches and programs that would take what I knew I was being called to do to the next level. I started an IAM movement for mothers and wives which turned into learning how to live a more fulfilled life; Beautiful

Living. I started going live on social media, afraid and all. I showed up twice a week giving tips and strategies on living a beautiful life, all while life was still happening in the background. I was still a mom and a wife, and it seemed the deeper I got with my purpose, the more chaos I was experiencing in my marriage.

One moment, my husband was encouraging me with my aspirations, and the next moment, he was telling me to figure it out by myself. There were moments of "I want a divorce" after every disagreement, and picking fights out of nowhere.

One day, frustrated, I left the house and cried out to God, saying, "God, why won't you make my marriage as beautiful as the things that I talk about?" When I returned, I got into bed and he immediately got out of bed and headed to the living room where I found him lying on the sofa. I wanted to know what was going on with him, so I went to the living room to talk, and during our conversation, I heard these words, "There comes a time in a man's life when he is unable to lead his family; he must leave to lead another one."

These words changed the trajectory of my life, indicating that my marriage was headed towards the brink of divorce. The revelation hit me hard, like a sudden bolt of lightning illuminating the dark clouds hovering over our marriage. In that moment, the path forward became a transformative journey, and these next seven chapters are the pillars that were born as I journeyed to living a more fulfilled life.

TWO

Mental Beauty

"For as he thinks in his heart, so is he."

Proverbs 23:7 (KJV)

Have you ever been in a space where it felt like your whole world was crashing and for the life of you, you couldn't see a way out? Every thought that came to you said that things would remain the same because of what you were seeing. Day in and day out you experienced sadness, confusion, insecurity, uncertainty, overwhelm, and worry. And perhaps you even felt like you were sinking in quicksand. What were your thoughts when you were in that space? Was it that you weren't good enough, or that your pain would never go away? Did you think, I won't ever be able to afford that house, I am stuck in this job, or this is just the life that

I was dealt? If you have ever been in that space or maybe you are in that space right now as you read this book, let me tell you that whatever you may be facing you can get through it with a healthy mindset.

Mental Beauty is the relationship that you have with your mind. Your mind is the gateway to what you want in life. Whether you think you can or think you can't all begins in your mind. Whether you are successful or not, and success can only be defined by you, all begins in your mind. Whether you believe that you are beautiful or deserve to live your best life, it all begins in your mind. Your mind is what determines which direction you will go in life and it's also what attracts things to you. If your mind focuses on negative things, you will attract negative things. If your mind focuses on positive things, you will attract positive things.

In 2017, I was faced with living on my own for the very first time in my life. My daughter and I had moved from my mom's place in 1999 to start life with my soon-to-be husband and he was moving from his grandmother's house so that we could become one family. After nearly 20 years of marriage, I was getting a divorce. It was scary. Trying to figure out what life would be like without him and find the perfect apartment that I felt would be safe and affordable.

It was August 2017 to be exact, I went searching for an apartment. I knew I didn't want to stay in a huge apartment community and I also knew that I wanted it to be gated. It needed to be something cute, and I needed to feel inclusive, and the area needed to feel safe. But I had no clue where to start or if I would find something that would allow me to stay near the same area where I was already living and be able to afford it on my own.

I walked into the leasing office and informed them that I needed a two-bedroom apartment. The staff was incredibly friendly and took me on a tour to see the different floor plans they had. I felt that it was the perfect location, it was a very small community, and I was able to afford it. I took a few days to consider the location and when I returned, I signed the lease, and it was for me to move in the following month. After signing the lease, I told about three people that I had found a place to stay but

I didn't utter a word to anyone else about finding an apartment. I was paralyzed by the thoughts of if I would be ok.

September came and I couldn't bring myself to move into my new apartment. I was afraid and all kinds of thoughts raced through my mind. This was new to me and I wondered if I could actually pull off living on my own. Would I be scared at night? Was it safe? And more importantly, is this the right place for me?

Terrified by the unknown, I tried to get out of the lease. I called the leasing office and explained that I had changed my mind, hoping that since I hadn't moved in yet, I could cancel the lease. Welp, that wasn't the case. They told me that I would have to pay money to get out of the place that I hadn't even stepped one foot into. I made a few phone calls to see if that was really the case and called a cousin to see if it was something that I could do legally, and it wasn't.

I began drowning in my thoughts and I had to do something. I had to check myself, otherwise, I was going to continue to spiral down a rabbit hole and that wasn't going to move me in the right direction. I had to shift my mindset and change how I was looking at things. The self-inflicted fears that I was putting out were hindering me from starting my new life.

So, I decided that instead of moving all at once, I would move things in a little at a time. I started with taking clothes and then one day, I decided that I would just go and sit and get acquainted with what was soon going to be my new beginning. Shifting my mindset was the best thing that I could do to successfully move forward given the situation that I was facing.

With no furniture in place, I often found myself sitting on the floor. However, I was usually in and out of the apartment very quickly. Then, one night as I was heading out the door of my apartment, I paused and looked around and found myself sliding down the wall crying out to God. At that moment, I asked that He give me peace that only He can give. I asked Him to watch over me every day as I entered and exited my apartment. I asked Him not to leave me and to be there with me. I cried and cried and suddenly, I felt peace and I knew I would be ok. I got up from the floor, wiped my face, and left.

It took me two months from the time that I signed my lease to move into my apartment. I knew I had to leave the place and person that I was so familiar with to start a new journey. I was stepping out into the unknown and it was scary, but I had peace. I had been allowing negative thinking to hold me hostage and keep me stuck.

I had to decide that I wasn't going to stay in that space and shift my mindset to an "I can do this" attitude and move forward in that direction. What I know is, life isn't always going to be easy, and even when you are experiencing a difficult season you must protect your mind and not allow negative thoughts. Sure, not-so-good things will happen from time to time and yes, the negative thoughts will come, but they don't have to stay. It's all up to you.

Negative thinking affects you mentally, emotionally, and physically. It paralyzes you and keeps you from living. Your mood and outlook on life are affected. You are stuck and it can cause you to hesitate to try something new. In my case, I was experiencing living on my own for the very first time. All the negative thinking delayed my move, but once I changed my perspective on the situation, I managed to overcome what was holding me back.

You may be in a difficult season right now and the negative thoughts are holding you captive, but you must decide at this very moment that you are going to change your mindset. Whether it's negative thoughts about your relationship, your health report, your children, or those thoughts that you have about yourself and how you are not good enough. Dwelling on negativity only keeps you stuck. It's time to break free from that cycle.

What you need to understand is that you are more than enough. There is Beautiful Living after divorce or whatever your trauma you may face, and ultimately, God has the final say regarding your children. Do what you can without losing yourself, pray for them, and entrust them to Him. Speak positivity over your health, ask lots of questions, and pray for healing and well-being.

Before I move on to the next pillar, I want to leave you with some strategies that can help you, change your mindset:

1. *Identify the source.* Take a moment to pinpoint where your negative thoughts are coming from. Your daily

influences such as people, social media, music, work environment, or even your living space, can impact your mindset. Once you have identified the source, replace it with something positive. This may look like changing your circle of friends, stepping back from a relationship, finding a new job, pursuing a fulfilling business venture, unfollowing negative influences on social media, or taking a break from it altogether. Clear your space: Clutter can contribute to scattered thoughts and negative energy. Take steps to declutter your physical environment, creating a space that promotes clarity and positivity. Regardless of the source, aim to replace negativity with positivity in your life.

2. *Talk it out.* Hun-ty, let me tell you something, sometimes you just need someone to talk to. When I was going through my divorce and facing a barrage of negative thoughts, it was nothing for me to phone a friend. I wore their ears out. In addition to my friends, I ended up with three therapists. So, don't hesitate to phone a friend and

if you find that negative thoughts are a recurring problem, find a therapist that you can talk to regularly. Talking allows you to release the thoughts you have and make room for positive ones.

3. *Write down your thoughts.* As I navigated through my separation and divorce, I turned to writing as a way to purge the negative thoughts from my mind. This allowed me to see how my thoughts were trapping me, but more importantly, it liberated me so that I could move forward.

4. *Find a way to serve others.* One way to deal with negative thoughts is to focus on helping someone else. After moving into my apartment, I found ways to help other people; it happened to be married couples. Seemingly, they drew to me. At first, I said, "Really God? You are sending people to me while I'm hurting?" Yet it turned out to be the best thing for me. It allowed me to focus on someone else instead of my negative thoughts and in turn, it brought positivity into my life.

5. *Affirmations*. Speaking affirmations over your life is a powerful tool for shifting your mindset. When I was going through my divorce, I strategically placed affirmations throughout my house. Now, I write affirmative statements for each area of my life and display them where I can see them daily. Affirmations can help boost your motivation and confidence. Each time you say an affirmation, you engage in positive self-talk, which gradually fosters a positive mindset. While it's not a magic bullet where your negative thoughts will automatically dissipate, consistently affirming yourself encourages your mind to embrace these positive statements as truth. When you truly believe you can do something, your actions often align accordingly.

Do this exercise: Write out a positive affirmation for every negative thought you are having in the present tense. Put them on sticky notes and place them in places that you see often. If you have a lamp with a lampshade in your bedroom, put them there and use the lampshade as a carousel and spin it when you need to redirect your thoughts. Write the affirmations on your bathroom mirror. Your bathroom is a place that you visit often and you can say them out loud when you are in there. Take about 3 minutes in the morning and at bedtime to affirm yourself. Repeat each affirmation about 5 times, focusing on the words that you are saying and believing what you are saying to be true.

Be consistent with speaking your affirmations daily and be patient with the process. Speaking affirmations over your life is a step toward change, but not the change itself. You still must do the work.

THREE

Spiritual Beauty

"I will show you what it's like when someone comes to me,

listens to my teaching, and then follows it. It is like a person

building a house who digs deep and lays the foundation on solid

rock. When the floodwaters rise and break against that house, it

stands firm because it is well built. But anyone who hears and

doesn't obey is like a person who builds a house right on the

ground, without a foundation. When the floods sweep down

against that house, it will collapse into a heap of ruins."

Luke 6:47-49 (NLT)

Imagine building your brand-new home on land that isn't solid.
The foundation is poured and the house goes up, but over a period
of time you began to have problems with your home. You notice
cracks in the exterior and interior walls, doors and windows are

difficult to close and if you have trees around your home, they begin to slump. You start to see a sunken area around the foundation and you failed to realize that your home was built on a sinkhole. What should you do? Run to God.

Before the house was built, a soil engineer should have been called to analyze the land. Much like life, people move through without consulting God and securing a sure foundation with Him.

Spiritual Beauty is the relationship that you have with God. It is the house that you are building. Matthew 7:24-27 says, "Therefore everyone who hears these words of mine and puts them into practice is like a wise man who built his house on the rock. The rain came down, the streams rose, and the winds blew and beat against that house; yet it did not fall, because it had its foundation on the rock. But everyone who hears these words of mine and does not put them into practice is like a foolish man who built his house on sand. The rain came down, the streams rose, and the winds blew and beat against that house, and it fell with a great crash." (NIV) So, are you building your life on the rock or on sand?

We must build our lives on the word of God to build a solid foundation with Him. Oftentimes something drastic must happen in our lives for us to turn to Him. It's in those times that we realize that our spiritual foundation has been compromised by shortcuts, thinking that we can do life by ourselves and then our whole world collapses under the stress of the winds and storms of life. Following God and submitting to His wisdom enables us to build a solid foundation based on God's values.

Having a relationship with God is the most important thing you can do in life. Scripture tells us that God knows the plans that He has for us (Jeremiah 29:11). And if He knows the plans that He has for us, and they are to prosper us and not to harm, then why wouldn't you want to make God the foundation of your life? God should be the first person you talk to when you wake. He should be the last person you talk to at night and in between times, God likes to chat too.

Having a strong foundation with God is the key to navigating life. I'm not implying that you won't have trials and tribulations because you will, but you will have Him to lean on as your solid rock and will be able to withstand whatever comes your way.

My relationship with God has been essential to my life, but I haven't always put Him first. When I was married, it was my family who consumed my days. I always heard this little still voice that said, "Don't forget about me." So, even in the chaos of life, I found myself saying, "Hey we need to go to church. Hey, we need to pray every night as a family. Husband, let's do bible study together right here in our home." But the one-on-one time that God longed to have with me was hit or miss outside of the praise and worship time that I had in the car nearly every day.

There were times when God had to sit me down to get my attention. As I mentioned earlier, I found myself doing the most in 2014 and knocked my hormones out of balance and the ONLY voice that I could stand to hear was the voice of the Lord. He spoke to me often during that time and answered questions that I had for Him and gave me visions of some things that would come to pass in my life.

Why does God have to allow things to happen to sit us down to talk to us? Why don't we automatically desire time with Him just like we desire time with our boo?

God isn't looking to take up the whole 24 hours in the day, but He does desire alone time with us. He longs to have a personal relationship with you. God knows the intimate details of our lives. Luke 12:7 tells us that He knows the number of hairs on our heads and that we are more important than the flock of sparrows. We are more important than anything else on earth.

God invites us to come to Him and to know Him (Revelations 22:17). When we desire to have an intimate relationship with Him, we will seek and thirst for Him (Psalm 63:1). Spending time alone with God frees our minds of distraction so that we can focus on Him and hear His voice.

Throughout the day, you can tell Him about how great your day is going or just pause to give thanks. Additionally, He wants us to pause and seek His thoughts about the business we want to start and how we are feeling about a challenging situation. He desires our most intimate moments with Him.

When you build a solid foundation with God, He becomes your life's compass. He will deepen your faith and teach you to discern his voice. For you to experience this, you must ensure that your foundation is maintained. You must invest your time. This will be unique to you and God and you must inspect the relationship often. To be sure that your spiritual foundation remains solid, you must dig your spiritual foundation deep.

After I moved into my apartment to prepare for my new life, I knew that I needed God more than ever. There were a lot of emotional days and nights. Sometimes I didn't know if I was coming or going. There were days that I didn't know how I got from point A to point B and back to point A, but I knew that God was right there with me. I felt Him. He was my life-support system. As I look back over those moments, I know that during those times, He was carrying me just like the *Footprints in the Sand* poem suggests.

During this period, I was able to discern God's voice and receive direction because I quieted my heart and embraced the still moments. You may be wondering why you haven't heard God's voice and I would say that it is because you may not have made room for Him in your life. You may be allowing the noise of the world to drown out His ever-so-meek voice or perhaps you hear Him but choose to ignore it because it's not what you want to hear. Besides the still, small whisper, you may discern His guidance through visions, a gut-feeling, or even dreams. For me, I experience God through visions and His small whisper, which are often confirmed by someone that has a close walk with Him.

This connection began because I desired a relationship with God and my heart longed for Him. Without a foundation built on God, I would have drowned trying to go through that experience alone.

Let's take a moment to take inventory of your relationship with God. So, when was the last time that you had a talk with Him? What steps can you take right now to deepen your relationship with Him? Consider the foundation of your relationship with God. Is it strong and secure, like a reinforced caisson, or is it fragile and vulnerable, like loose soil that may crack under pressure? Is your relationship with God balanced or does it feel one-sided? Do you only seek Him in times of trouble, or do you talk to Him when things are good too? Do you invite Him into your space and your daily activities? Do you consciously invite Him into your daily activities and spaces, or is He only on your mind sporadically? Reflecting on these questions can help you assess and strengthen your relationship with God.

Here are a few things that you can do to start building a strong foundation with God:

1. *Spend time with God.* Decide when you will spend time with God. As I mentioned earlier, God desires alone time with you. I recommend giving Him your first. When you wake, before you check social media and get the children together, spend time with God. This may require you to get up a little earlier to make this happen, but if this does not work for you, find

another time in your day when you can spend time
alone with Him.

2. *Connect with other believers.* The company you keep
   is essential. Bad company corrupts good character (1
   Corinthians 15:33-34), so you have to be careful
   about who you spend time with. Take inventory of the
   relationships in your life and spend time with those
   who are also seeking God. I call this community. This
   community can help you be consistent and grow in
   character, wisdom, and understanding. It will also
   help you to get a perspective that you may not be able
   to discover on your own. Additionally, when hard
   times come, which they will, you'll have your
   community to turn to for support and to help get you
   through.

3. *Fellowship with other believers.* Find a local church
   that you can attend to worship and hear His word.
   Worshipping, for me, is everything. I have said time
   and time again that worship is the best part of the

service to me. Not that I don't get anything from the message that is being delivered, but it's like becoming one with the Lord. It's just me and Him and my imperfect vocals, but during that time it's the most melodious sound that you could ever hear. Being planted in a local church allows you to meet other people and get involved so that you can serve and it helps you to grow and mature spiritually and use your spiritual gifts. Since being part of my church, I have connected with the souls of fellow members, I have grown in my prayer life, I received my heavenly language, and I also serve in the women's ministry where I facilitate and teach classes using my gift of encouragement.

4. *Faith.* Trusting God and obeying and applying His word is crucial to building a solid foundation of faith. When storms of life come your way, you'll be grounded in biblical truth and remain steady as a rock. People often claim they have faith, but it's not always easy to walk it

out when God calls you to adjust your life and obey.

Faith is the unseen, requiring us to trust in God's wisdom

and timing even when we can't see the outcome.

Therefore, it's essential to build a solid foundation of

faith, rooted in Scripture and prayer, so that when God

speaks, we are ready to move without hesitation,

knowing His plans are perfect.

Build your foundation on God so when life happens, which

it will, (the divorce, the health challenges, the death of a loved

one, your finances in shambles, the loss of a job, your children

out of control, and all the other things that can happen) you

would have built your life on a solid foundation that can

withstand all the trials and tribulations of life.

FOUR

Physical Beauty

"Or do you not know that your body is a temple of the Holy Spirit within you, whom you have from God? You are not your own, for you were bought with a price. So glorify God in your body."

1 Corinthians 6:19-20 (ESV)

Physical Beauty is not about how tall or short you are, your eye color or whether your hair is long or short. It has nothing to do with aesthetics. I wanted to get that out of the way. Physical beauty is the relationship that you have with your body and how well you take care of it. It's what you're eating, it's the condition of your body, it's whether you are putting proper nutrients in your body and doing some form of physical activity, and it's whether you are getting enough sleep. It's doing the things that you love that keep you mentally, physically, and emotionally well. It's self-care. Physical beauty is critical for living longer and your overall well-being. Poor physical health can influence your mental and emotional health and overall life.

Physical and mental beauty goes hand in hand. When you are overly emotional for a period of time, stressed, and not properly taking care of yourself, it will affect your mind and your body. Your mind can become lethargic and foggy. It can feel like a matrix out of control in your head.

I know a thing or two about this because in 2014, I experienced it. I was walking around with an invisible "S" on my chest that stood for superwoman. As mentioned in chapter one, I was working a full-time job, doing hair part-time, a full-time dance mom, mentoring at-risk juvenile boys at the church, and running a multi-level marketing business with a team, plus I was a wife and mother all at the same time. My friends would often ask me how I was doing all the things that I was doing. I adopted the nickname "Superwoman" from them. My response would often be, I don't think about it, I just keep moving.

I didn't have time to work out, wait let me rephrase that... I didn't *make* time to work out because I felt that my plate was already full. I was often eating fast food or whatever was prepared at the house in addition to sugar. I was running on fumes and didn't even know it until one day I decided to get some good old peach mango tea from Piccadilly Cafeteria. Don't act like y'all don't know about the dilly. It was good and then I decided to have a bite-size snicker. All of a sudden, my brain felt like it was doing etch-a-sketch in my head. I wasn't sure what was going on at the time, but I knew what I was feeling and experiencing wasn't right.

Shortly after experiencing this, I was asked a question that I clearly knew the answer to but at the moment, my mind was blank, and I couldn't pull the answer out of my head. I phoned my husband to ask him the question that was being asked of me and he answered it and said, "You didn't remember that?" I told him that something wasn't feeling right in my head and that I couldn't remember. By nightfall, listening to my family's voice became an irritant so much so that I dismissed myself from the dinner table because my mind was still feeling like an etch-a-sketch.

I went and laid down on the bed calling out to God. I knew something wasn't right and that's all I knew to do. I put on some gospel music and had it turned down low and to my surprise, I could listen to it. I hummed the songs to distract myself from the matrix activity that was happening in my brain.

The next morning, I experienced the same thing and made a call to my doctor to be seen. No one could figure out what was going on with me. For a couple of weeks, I was incapacitated not able to do much for myself. I became frustrated that after going to doctor after doctor, no one could figure out what was going on. I was told that I needed to rest and get some sleep. While it may have been true that I needed rest and sleep, I couldn't shake the feeling that there was more to it than just physical exhaustion. I mean, I couldn't even listen to my children's voices. Besides some light gospel music, the house had to be completely silent. I could feel the fear trying to creep in that I would remain in that state forever and that I wouldn't get better.

Nobody could understand why I was walking through the house mumbling while my brain was racing. I couldn't explain what was happening, but I knew that whatever it was, it was forcing me to sit down and be still.

God laid it on my heart to do my own research. I found out that I had a condition called Premenstrual Dysphoric Disorder (PMDD) and I had a severe case of it. I knocked my hormones completely out of balance because I wasn't practicing self-care. I felt depressed and irritable, I had trouble concentrating, a lack of interest in doing anything, and I felt overwhelmed and out of control. There were moments when anxiety and panic attacks took over.

Not only did I have to sit down and be still, but I was mostly bedridden. I could no longer drive because being in the car made me feel extremely claustrophobic. Imagine being in that state for weeks and not knowing if you would get better.

When I tell you that my house was as quiet as a mouse. My children spoke to one another with a whisper. My husband at the time tried his best to care for me not knowing what to do but making sure that I was comfortable. When I got lethargic, I would get up and pace the floor and talk to myself. That was an indicator that I needed to eat. He would rush down to the kitchen and whip up the quickest meal.

I can remember one time that it got so bad that I grabbed a pair of scissors and attempted to cut my hair. My oldest daughter had come home from college and happened to be walking behind me as I raised my hand to cut a twist that I had in my hair. She grabbed my arm and removed the scissors. I told her that I wanted the twists out and that I wanted to go outside and walk in the street. She hollered to her dad to hurry with the food.

That was a hard lesson for me. I had to make a change and do something that I hadn't done before. I had to slow down and pay more attention to what was going on in my world. I had run myself ragged, as many of us do, and it was time to eliminate some things from my life and do things differently. I left the hair salon and I took my daughter out of competitive dancing because she was practicing six sometimes seven days a week. I stopped mentoring the at-risk juvenile boys and I walked away from the MLM business.

I began going to my neighborhood park to walk and jog to release some feel-good endorphins. I also went to group therapy and started journaling and spending more time with God. I often sat in my brown leather chair near the window with the blinds up listening to the birds chirping, God speaking, and writing. I decided to put myself first and take care of myself. Had that not happened for me, I probably would still be running through life like a chicken with my head cut off. Sadly, it took me knocking my hormones out of balance for me to refocus and find balance, prioritize self-care in my life, and to stop making everything so urgent.

I began eating more home-cooked meals and by 2016, I had changed my diet by not consuming beef, pork, and chicken and having sugar in moderation. I realized that the foods that I was eating were not good for me and were contributing to my hormonal imbalance. I am mostly a pescatarian/plant-based eater now. Even with that, I still incorporate some type of physical exercise for my bone health and mental sanity. However, sometimes self-motivation isn't present. Recognizing that working out isn't my forte, I decided to enlist a workout partner to hold me accountable and have someone else do the same.

Running around with the "S" on our chest is not the only time we can find ourselves in comprising situations with our health. When you experience grief, that can impact your physical health. Separating from my husband was a very traumatic experience and I found myself losing weight even though I was eating. My doctor told me that I had turned off the chemical (leptin) that would tell my body to gain weight. So, you mean to tell me that I was able to turn this chemical off then, but now I can't... ok, that was a sidebar.

But not being in a good emotional state can take a toll on your body. I found myself losing weight, struggling to get proper sleep, and neglecting regular exercise. Despite these challenges, I still had to take care of my baby girl, who was just in middle school at the time. When it was my turn to have her, I had to dig deep and find healthy ways to cope with the emotional turmoil.

I got a support system. My support system consisted of God, my friends, three therapists, the billboard that said, "Everything Will Be Ok," and whoever crossed my path in the streets that listened. Now, of course, I just didn't walk up to people and vomit what I was going through, it was God-led. I also made weekend plans ahead of time so that I wouldn't find myself balled up in a knot in the corner of a room. I learned to be ok with dating myself and had my around-the-clock counselors and friends that I could call on at any time.

Whether you are a mom, a wife, or a caregiver who has devoted so much of your time to your loved ones and forgotten about yourself, know that you need to take some time to take care of YOU. More times than none, you are last on the priority list or you feel guilty for doing things for yourself and that shouldn't be. Putting yourself on top of your to-do list isn't a crime and could mean less stress, better health, and a better overall quality of life.

You must find the time to relax and de-stress to avoid throwing your hormones off balance as I did and to protect your mental health. Relaxation will allow your mind and body to repair itself and in turn you will make better decisions. Oh, honey, I can hear you now, "I just don't have time." Ok, well schedule it into your busy day just like you do everything else. If you can't find a whole hour for yourself, then break it up. Do a 15-minute walk after lunch, a 15-minute walk after dinner, spend some time with friends, ask for help and find time to laugh often.

This is important and shouldn't be taken lightly. If you can't give yourself the care you need, how are you going to be any good for anyone else? You are to operate from your overflow, the full cup belongs to you.

Maybe you are going through a divorce or experiencing the death of a loved one, or facing some other type of grief. Know that depression and stress are real, and you shouldn't try to go through it alone. Or maybe you are running through life with the "S" on your chest, being there for everyone else and not taking care of yourself first. For the sake of your health and to become the best version of yourself for others, you must make some changes and take action now.

Here are some strategies to follow if you are grieving:

1. First, allow yourself the time needed to grieve. Get a good support system consisting of people you can lean on who can provide emotional support during this time.

2. Schedule time to eat. Put an alarm on your phone if needed to remind you to eat.

3. Take time to walk. Not only will it release those feel-good endorphins that I mentioned earlier, but it will be a good way to get fresh air and clear your mind.

4. Invest in a life coach who has gone through a divorce or a grief counselor to help you get through this transition. But hear me when I say this, it is crucial to take time to breathe, sit with your emotions and acknowledge where you are in your healing process. Remember, you don't have to go through this alone. Seek support from friends, family, or support groups as well, as having a supportive network can make the journey easier.

5. Decide how long you will stay in that space. For instance, at some point, I realized that I was tired of being in that space, so I started putting myself on a

timer. It started with 15 minutes, then 10 minutes, and then 5 minutes, and then 1 minute and I had to get up and do something else. So, set the timer and when it goes off, you must get up and do a hobby that you love. You can't stay in that space. Take whatever steps necessary to care for yourself and be sure to give yourself grace along the way.

Here are ways to slow down and take time for yourself:

1. *De-clutter your schedule.* Take a look at your weekly schedule and determine what's important and what can be delegated to someone else. Identify those things that you can eliminate from your plate altogether.

2. *Schedule your "me-time."* Set time aside just for you. This isn't the time to catch up on household chores, spend time with your boo, or attend to your children or pets. This time is solely for doing what brings you joy, without any external expectations. Allocate this time weekly or bi-weekly for a personal date and incorporate *daily* moments for self-care.

3. *Express your needs.* Expressing your needs is a crucial aspect of maintaining healthy relationships and personal well-being. It involves open communication and setting clear boundaries to ensure that your needs are met. No one else can accurately guess or understand what you require, so it becomes your responsibility to articulate those needs to the people around you. If you need alone time, it's essential to communicate this to your friends and family. By expressing your desire for solitude, you create a space for self-care and reflection. This practice not only fosters a better understanding of your own needs but also allows your loved ones to respect and support your boundaries.

4. *Set boundaries.* Setting boundaries is a form of self-care. In the process of supporting others, you might stretch yourself too thin and experience burnout. I expressed earlier in this chapter how I knocked my hormones completely out of whack by doing the most. I had no boundaries. This resulted in burnout, compromised

mental health, and a significant decline in productivity. It was a stark reminder of the importance of establishing and respecting personal boundaries to safeguard my well-being. Setting boundaries involves clearly defining what you are comfortable with, learning to say no when necessary, and prioritizing self-care. It's a proactive step in preserving your physical and emotional well-being, ensuring that you have the capacity to support others effectively without sacrificing your own needs.

5. *Learn to say no.* Your time is precious and if there is something that you just don't want to do then say no. Time is limited and one thing that you cannot get back. Use it to do things that you want to do. I know saying no can be difficult, so practice saying no to the little things first. For instance, you could say no when someone requires your immediate attention while you are headed to the shower. Unless it's an emergency, it can wait for to you take your precious time in the shower and address their needs afterward.

6. *Eat well.* Eating well requires careful planning. Without taking the time to plan our meals, we may find ourselves resorting to fast-food options that are often unhealthy. This can lead to consuming foods high in sugar and saturated fats, contributing to potential skin issues and other health concerns. If you are like most and don't have time in the morning to prepare breakfast and lunch before you go out the door, meal-prepping can be a valuable solution. When I meal prep, it saves me time, money, and frustration of trying to figure out what I want to eat at the last minute. It also helps me manage my weight as I get to decide the ingredients I want to use and my portion size. You can prepare your meals the night before so that you can grab them and go the next morning. If your nights are long, then choose a day that works best for you, perhaps a Sunday, and prepare your meals in containers so that you can grab and go during the week or hire someone that can prepare a certain

number of meals for you if time doesn't permit for you to do it yourself.

7. *Exercise*. Ok, so I'm not implying that you must go to a gym if you don't like the gym. You can go to the park or you can exercise in your home. The most important thing is for you to find a form of exercise that you enjoy and do it. This is a great way to spend time with yourself unless you are like me and like to work out with other people. Aim to do some form of exercise at least three times a week and if you need an accountability partner then ask a friend to join you. Make sure to schedule this time on your calendar when you are planning out your week. Having an exercise routine can greatly improve your physical health and well-being.

So, what changes do you need to make in your life? What do you need to eliminate from your to-do list so that you can take better care of yourself? How's your diet? Who do you need to become to achieve these goals? Taking care of yourself is a daily decision. You only have one life, one temple. Eat well, exercise,

slow down, and practice self-care so that you may live longer.

FIVE

Relational Beauty

"A new command I give you: Love one another. As I

have loved you, so you must love one another."

John 13:34 (NIV)

Having and cultivating healthy relationships is crucial to your well-being. Relational Beauty is the core pillar of Beautiful Living. It's the relationship that you have with yourself first and then the relationship you have with others. Cultivating healthy relationships with yourself and others is essential to life.

The relationship that you have with yourself is vital because it is the foundation for all your other relationships. The stronger your relationship with yourself, the better your relationship can be with others. When your self-relationship is healthy, you value who you are and embrace what you've experienced. It takes self-awareness, self-acceptance, and self-care to be able to have a healthy relationship with yourself. This self-relationship also affects your mind, your relationship with God, your body, your finances, whether you will operate in purpose, and how you show up for what God has called you to do.

To cultivate a positive self-relationship, you must reduce negative self-talk, have a healthy relationship with your body, check in with your mental health, spend time with the people you love, take care of your emotional needs, do things that you enjoy, and operate in your purpose. And for the record, taking time to love yourself is not selfish, it's necessary because it not only aids in your personal growth, but it also improves the relationship that you have with others.

Additionally, you can see clearly where you are and where you would like to be. It is impossible to be emotionally available to others if you aren't connected and emotionally available to yourself first.

When I was going through my divorce, there were people who repeatedly told me to go out on a date in order for me to move on from my soon-to-be ex. Are you kidding me? One, I was nowhere near emotionally available for anyone to be in my space, so dating was off the table. My ability to recognize this was self-awareness. I knew the state that I was in emotionally and I would have been wasting someone's son's time.

Two, after being with someone as long as I had been with him, moving past him wasn't going to happen that quickly. Oh, but I gave them a word or two about it and told them if they mentioned it to me again, they wouldn't be able to talk to me anymore. I didn't need the pressure of moving on and had to set a boundary around that. I knew they were just trying to help but I was not in that space at that time. When you are emotionally unavailable, you should not try to foster a relationship with anyone. Instead, take time and heal from whatever happened to put you in that state.

This brings me to the relationship that you have with others. I am one to say that I love to love people and I love meeting new people and developing new relationships. My family and friends often joke that everyone I meet is my friend and that I never meet a stranger. Over the years, I've formed lasting friendships with women I've met while out shopping, and to this day, we remain connected. I am thankful for my tribe and I am surely blessed to have had them while I was going through my divorce and the aftermath of it. Divorce can be messy and it usually hurts a lot of people because along the way you both created friendships together and those connections usually end when your marriage does. But I'm grateful for the ones who stayed by my side.

During this time in my life, I experienced emotions that I didn't even know existed. Divorce felt worse than death to me. The betrayal, manipulation, gaslighting, suicidal thoughts…wait, I won't just skip past that part. As much as I wish those thoughts didn't occur, they did. Sometimes grief can have you to come to a point where you do not feel that life is worth living. The pain was overwhelming, something that I had never experienced before. I had to remember who I was. I had a good self-relationship and tapped into taking care of myself. Although I had a tribe, I still needed to know how to be there for myself in the event they couldn't be in my time of need.

Developing a good self-relationship throughout my life was pivotal during this time. That's why it's so important that you learn who you are and then love, accept, and take care of yourself. Relationships are mutual commitments despite the role the other person plays in your life. You should treat others how you want to be treated and treat yourself how you want others to treat you. I believe that you teach others how to treat you, and what you attract is a direct reflection of who you are at the time. You should evaluate the relationships in your life often. Sometimes we hold on to people that we need to get let go of.

As you grow, some people will need to be left behind they no longer serve the position in your life that they once did. Holding on to those people past their expiration date may prevent you from reaching your next God-level, and until you free yourself of them, you may remain stagnant; not reaching your full potential. In relationships, it's important that you grow together, but as the saying goes, people come into your life for a reason, a season, or a lifetime.

The Reason. When someone enters your life for a reason, it's often to fulfill a need – be it emotional, spiritual, or physical – that you've expressed, either inwardly or outwardly. This person has come to assist you during a difficult time, to support and guide you, or to enhance your overall well-being. They may seem like a blessing, and indeed, they are. They are present precisely when you need them most. Then, without you doing anything wrong or at an inconvenient moment, circumstances lead to the end of the relationship. It's crucial to recognize that their purpose has been fulfilled, and their role in your life is complete. The prayer you sent up has been answered, and it is now time to move on.

I met new people while going through my divorce that had experienced what I was going through. I did feel as if they were godsent because none of my female friends in my inner circle could relate to my experience. Many of those people who came to assist me during that difficult time are no longer in contact. There were no hard feelings; they came to do what they were sent to do, which was help me to get through or share their experiences. Over time, the talking dissipated, perhaps as I was healing and growing from the marriage.

The Season. Not all relationships are meant to last a lifetime. Throughout life, you should take a moment to evaluate your relationships and realize those that are not meant to be with you forever. Things change. What initially brought you together either becomes not enough to keep the relationship growing, or you realize that your aspirations diverge, and your paths no longer align. Perhaps there were valuable lessons or experiences meant to be shared, or personal growth that needed to occur. While these relationships may have brought you joy and fulfillment, it's essential to acknowledge when it's time to move forward.

In some cases, relationships serve a specific purpose, much like my interactions with clients. I am brought into their lives to provide guidance and direction. Without clarity of purpose, one merely exists. Thus, I step in as their co-pilot for a defined period, assisting them in navigating towards their desired destination.

The Lifetime. A lifelong friend is someone you connect with and expect to remain friends forever. This doesn't necessarily mean that you will see or talk to them every day. Someone who knows you, and who you know, and you mutually accept each other for who you are, and make time for each other as needed. I am blessed to have two amazing best friends. One of them, my longest-standing relationship, is someone I've known since sixth grade. We met in middle school, and she helped me to see clearly during my sixth-grade year. I needed glasses, and for the life of me, I don't know why I didn't have them. I didn't get them until ninth grade. However, she had multiple pairs and generously shared them with me, bringing the ones she wasn't wearing for me to use during the school day.

We began coordinating our clothes to match the color glasses that we were going to wear each day. She would let me know what color she was wearing so I could wear something different to match the other pair of glasses. I really didn't care if they matched or not; I was just happy that she was thoughtful enough to share them with me at school.

We went to the eighth-grade prom together, although we didn't match. She wore a peach-colored knee-length fitted dress, while I wore a long purple Cinderella-like dress with sequin at the top. But we did have the same earrings that matched the color of our dresses. I spent the night at her house a lot and often hung out on the weekends at the skating rink where we were only there to dance. We would stand at the dance room door like the people in the Upton's commercial and be like, open, open, open, and would dance until the lights came on.

We ended up going to different high schools and we didn't hang out as much, but still referred to one another as best friends. After high school, we stayed in touch, but I ended up getting married early and she remained single, living a totally different life. I had a whole husband and kids while it appeared that she was out living her single best life. There were years that went by that I didn't speak to her at all, but I still considered her my best friend and she was always in my heart. When we did talk, we just picked up where we left off, and it was apparent that our love for one another never changed. Fast forward to today, we talk regularly, we are there for one another, and I cherish the time that we spend together, affirming that our love remains steadfast and solid.

My other best friend came into my life during adulthood. We met at work, sharing the same floor and eventually finding ourselves on the same team. Initially, our interactions were marked by my persistent engagement with her, much to her initial dismay. She humorously recalls trying to avoid me because I had a knack for drawing her into conversations when she craved solitude. Despite her attempts to maintain her own space, I somehow managed to break through her shell.

Our friendship took a turn when I invited her on a cruise for my aunt's wedding, and to my surprise, she accepted. Since then, she's been a steadfast presence in my life, standing by me through the highs and lows, from divorce and surgeries to doctor's appointments. Despite my occasional jokes that she's free to retreat into her shell, she firmly rejects the notion, stating that I'm stuck with her for life.

You may not have two best friends or even one, having sisters or close friends who feel like sisters is incredibly special. However, even if you don't have biological sisters or a large circle of friends, nurturing a deep connection with just one friend can be incredibly fulfilling.

To cultivate healthy, long-standing friendships, you must first learn how to be a friend. Learn how to give compliments, support them, be a good listener, be trustworthy, have empathy, make time for them, maintain respect for one another, and love what makes you guys different. Relationships are an indispensable ingredient in a happy life, so be sure to give them the care and attention they deserve.

Whether you have sisters, friends, or both, the bonds you cultivate are invaluable sources of love, support, and companionship throughout life's journey. I am thankful for both of my best friends, my relationships with my beautiful sisters, and the close friendships that I have. I cherish their unwavering support and the countless moments of laughter we've shared along the way.

In addition to nurturing healthy relationships with others, be sure to prioritize the growth of your personal self-relationship. It's important that you check in with yourself regularly to assess your emotions and thoughts. It's not enough to simply acknowledge that you're "feeling some type of way" without digging deeper into the specific emotions you are experiencing. Identifying these feelings accurately allows you to take appropriate course of action to address them and improve your well-being. Furthermore, cultivating a healthy self-relationship is a gradual journey and not an overnight achievement. It requires patience and understanding with yourself as you navigate through various experiences and emotions.

Here are some other things that you can do to foster a healthy self-relationship:

1. *Forgive yourself.* We all make mistakes in life and when we do, it's important to have some compassion for yourself and forgive yourself. Forgiving yourself leads to better mental and emotional well-being, and it frees you from suffering. You will have more peace and healthier relationships when you learn to forgive yourself.

2. *Embrace your uniqueness.* Celebrate the qualities that set you apart and make you special. Acknowledge and accept both your strengths and weaknesses, and recognize that they are all part of what makes you unique. Embracing yourself fully allows for a deeper connection with others.

3. *Set boundaries.* I mentioned setting boundaries in the previous chapter. You can see how setting boundaries is important in different areas of your life. It overlaps your mental and physical health with your self-relationship. Learn to say no when necessary and communicate your needs effectively. It helps to create a clear standard of how you would like to be treated and let others know what's acceptable and what's not. Setting boundaries helps protect your well-being and fosters positive relationships. So, set them. They are for you and your peace of mind.

4. *Journal.* Journaling is a powerful tool for self-reflection. It has always been a great tool to empty my mind and a

great way to express my feelings. It is therapeutic for me, and helps me to become one with myself. The essence of journaling lies in embracing imperfection; there's no right or wrong way… write or draw whatever comes to mind, following what feels best for you.

5. *Say positive affirmations.* I can't say enough how speaking positive things about yourself makes a difference in your overall well-being. No, it's not a magic wand that will make everything that you may be feeling disappear, but it will help you to overcome negative thoughts that you may have about yourself. Reciting daily positive affirmations will help to minimize negativity and help you to see yourself in a positive light. When a negative thought comes to mind, replace it with a positive affirmation.

6. *Treat yourself.* Treat yourself to things that bring you joy. Whether that's to a movie, a nice solo dinner, ice cream, buying yourself some flowers, or even the spa. As long as it's not going to put you in debt, do it. You

deserve it. Do things for yourself that you expect others to do for you.

7. *Invest in a life coach and/or therapist.* Invest in a life coach to help you with the vision for your life, set goals and strategies and a plan to execute them, or go and see a therapist if you are struggling with some past trauma and see that you cannot move forward.

Remember, cultivating relationships starts with making sure that your relationship with yourself is healthy so that you may be able to cultivate other healthy relationships.

SIX

Financial Beauty

"Bring the whole tithe into the storehouse, that there may be

food in my house. Test me in this," says the LORD Almighty,

"and see if I will not throw open the floodgates of heaven and

pour out so much blessing that there will not be room enough to

store it."

Malachi 3:10 (NIV)

I can remember it like it was yesterday, it was payday, and after paying my tithes first and then all of my other bills, I was left with $3.27. It was the Friday before Spring Break in 2019 and I had to go and get my daughter from her dads so that she could spend spring break with me. I had no groceries in the house and no money to do anything with my daughter over the break. All I had was enough gas to go around the corner to pick her up.

But before leaving out the door, I cried out to God and said, "God, I have done what you've asked. You said to give my first tenth, and I did. I have been faithful; I've been tithing. I gave it to you before I even paid my rent and I paid all my bills. And now I'm left with $3.27, and I have to go and get your daughter, and there's no food in the house, and I won't be able to do anything with her."

After calling out to God I sat still at my kitchen table in silence. One tear fell and I said, "I can't cry because you told me that you are my provider. You are my husband right now and you're everything that I need. So, you're going to have to talk to me and tell me what I need to do."

Suddenly, I had this "aha" moment and it was like God reminding me that he gave me a gift and a talent and to use my hands. I remembered at that moment that there were people who had been asking me to do their hair. Because I had no desire to do hair anymore, I had been saying no when asked and stopped doing it. I remembered a cousin who had asked last, and she asked me to think about it so I sent her a text message asking if she still wanted her hair done and she said yes. I scheduled her for the next day.

And then, out of the blue, a friend of mine sent me some money without me asking. I sent another message to a friend, telling them that I was going to get my daughter and that she was going to need some spring break money. Without question or hesitation, I received another $100. I had enough money to get groceries, take her to the Aquarium, and to Candytopia. We had the best time ever that week and still had money left over.

Financial Beauty is the relationship that we have with money. Reflecting on that pivotal moment, I recognized the divine presence of God amidst my financial struggles. Within an hour, things were turned around. He showed me very quickly how He had gone before me and that He had not left me or forsaken me (Deuteronomy 31:8). This experience reaffirmed my belief that God is our ultimate provider and will supply all of our needs (Philippians 4:19). It emphasized the importance of developing a deep relationship with Him, trusting in His guidance, and having faith in His provision. He desires to care for His children, understanding the essential role money plays in our lives.

Amidst my financial uncertainties, I had been wrestling with the idea of moving to my mom's house. It had been vacant for about two years and she mentioned me living in her home after I had already moved into my apartment, so I said, "No." A year went by and she mentioned it again saying that she wanted to fix it up and asked if I would move into it. I really didn't want to because I loved where I was living and thought that it would bring too many memories since it was near my home where I once lived with my then-husband. I also felt things getting tight financially and couldn't figure out why but after that pivotal moment of having only $3.27 left, I felt a divine nudge, prompting me to contemplate my next steps. With five months left on my lease, I took some time to think about it. I moved, trusting in God's guidance for my future path.

One of the things that I wanted to consistently be able to do was tithe and pay off bills. Moving to my mom's house afforded me the opportunity to consistently tithe and pay off some bills. God has asked that we give our first fruits to Him (Proverbs 3:9-10), which means sacrificing something that costs us a little. It means putting God first, even before ourselves, or our family. Giving a tenth of your income first before doing anything else is a way to show that we trust God with our lives and our finances. After separating from my husband, I stopped tithing, it just didn't seem like I had enough to do so. I was sad about it because I had a deep desire to tithe as I had before and start a small group with the church in my home. Well since I wasn't a tither, I wasn't eligible to start a small group in the church. I decided to trust God. I changed my mindset, gave to God first, then paid my rent, and then paid the remainder of my bills. So, when I only had $3.27 left, I was surprised because I hadn't experienced that in previous months. Truthfully, I think I low-key wanted to see if God would really take care of me and, as I mentioned at the beginning of this chapter, He was right there when I didn't see a way. He opened my eyes and reminded me that He had me and that He would provide for me and not forsake me. Tithing isn't for God because of course, He doesn't need our money. It's for our benefit to sacrifice a portion of our income which is a constant reminder to rely on God to meet our needs.

When you go through a divorce, your finances are affected by it. It can put you in debt as you have to cover attorney fees, bills that you're left with, the cost of starting over and the list goes on. Debt affects your life financially, emotionally, mentally, and physically. It can cause anxiety, depression, and mental illness; not to mention the strain that it can put on your family. This may not be the reason for your debt, but not having the discipline to not shop when you don't have the money might be. Buying expensive things like cars, houses, purses, and red bottoms that have you living paycheck to paycheck so that you stay tied to a job that you hate for a lifestyle that you truly can't afford isn't the best way to live. By no means is this judgment. I haven't bought any red bottoms because I don't want my feet to hurt, but I have swiped a credit card to buy a lot of clothes which lead to a cluttered closet, anxiety, feeling depressed, and no room to put it all.

The Good News. The good news is that God wants to bless us abundantly (2 Corinthians 9:8). He knows our every need and our every desire. Oftentimes, financially, we are where we are because of disobedience, mishandling money (living beyond our means), and not moving when he's trying to redirect our path because we are trying to hold on to the little bit that we have because it feels "safe." God is saying to us, He will open up the gates of heaven and pour out a blessing that we won't have enough room to receive it all (Malachi 3:10) if we would just trust Him and His guidance and move when He says to move.

God came that we may have life and have it to the full (John 10:10) and lack no good thing (Psalm 34:10) but we must trust Him and follow His guidance. He wants us to be the head and not the tail and the lender and not the borrower (Deuteronomy 28:10-13).

Here are some tips that can aid you on your journey to having financial beauty:

1. *Don't compare yourself with others.* It's natural to desire things that others have, but trying to keep up with the

Joneses has never been a good idea. This pursuit can lead you to spend money that you don't have, resulting in credit card debt. Avoid comparing your possessions to what others have. If you want it, work towards it by saving, getting better job opportunities, or starting a side hustle; but do not go into debt for it. The act of comparison can trigger feelings of depression and anxiety, which is not how God intended for you to live. Instead, practice gratitude for what you already have and set realistic goals to attain your desires without accumulating credit card debt or living paycheck to paycheck. Focus on competing with who you are right now against the person you aspire to become.

2. *Identify and cut emotional spending.* Do you buy things when you are feeling down to make you feel better or do you buy things when you're feeling extremely happy? Pay attention when you shop to identify the triggers that lead to impulse to shop, especially when you don't have the funds to do so. Personally, I found myself shopping

when I felt extremely happy. However, since the pandemic, I haven't done nearly the amount of shopping that I did in the past (thank God!) mainly because I don't enjoy going to the malls anymore and the stores I used to frequent closed. Now when I feel extremely happy and, in some cases, bored, I pull out my computer and visit what used to be my favorite store and peruse the online site. Because shopping online is a different experience for me, I have found myself not doing hardly any emotional spending as I'm not as eager to buy. I can't touch and feel the items, and I'm unsure how it's going to look on me. As a result, I often let things sit in the cart for days or even weeks. Either I forget about them, or by the time I remember to go back, the items are either gone, and I'm like, "Oh well," or if they're still there, I no longer have the desire to buy them. Many times, I've realized that I needed to perform the act of putting things in the cart, and since I don't check out right away, I usually find that the initial urge to buy has passed, and I won't go back for it. Waiting 24 hours has helped me avoid impulsive spending triggered by feeling down or the need to fulfill the desire for something to do. Be sure to recognize your shopping triggers and set a budget for things that are not a necessity.

3. *Forgive yourself for past financial mistakes.* Everyone makes mistakes so forgive yourself for any previous money-related missteps. However, it's crucial not to forget these mistakes. Remembering is essential for growth and will help you avoid repeating the same mistakes, contributing to building a positive mindset. Allow those past financial missteps to be lessons that guide you toward making different choices in the future.

4. *Create a spending plan.* Creating a spending plan was a little difficult for me to do at first. I wasn't accustomed to it, but as I grew a little wiser, I realized that it was best for me to do so. I use an excel spreadsheet and in one column I put the name of every company that I pay each month. In the second column, I put the amount, and

then in the third column, I put when that bill is due. Be sure that you don't forget to add a line for groceries and gas. Be patient as you create your spending plan. There may be some trial and error in the beginning because some of your bills may fluctuate from month to month. Check to see if your utilities can be put on a budget plan so that you can know how much those bills will be each month. Having a spending plan can help you track where your money goes each month and how much you have left to save and treat yourself if you so choose to.

5. *Find financial coaches and mentors and seek guidance.* A good financial coach can help you set up your budget, get out of debt, and assist you with setting your financial goals. Additionally, they can provide valuable insights on investing, saving, and building a secure financial future.

You are in control of your finances. You decide what to buy and what not to buy. You even have control over how much money you make. If you're not making enough, then do something about it. Seeking a positive money mindset can help you feel better about yourself, and it can also help you reach your financial goals. Remember, God will not withhold any good thing from you (Psalm 84:11).

SEVEN

Professional Beauty

"For I know the plans I have for you," declares the Lord,

"plans to prosper you and not to harm you, plans to give you

hope and a future."

Jeremiah 29:11 (NIV)

God is calling. How will you answer? Jeremiah 1:5 tells us that before we were formed in our mother's womb, he knew us, before we were born, he set us apart. Just as He appointed Jeremiah as a prophet to the nations, we were intentionally created with purpose. Each of us carries a unique purpose that beckons us to step into the field of action aligned with His calling. So, what is God calling you to do?

Professional Beauty is operating in the purpose that God is calling you to do. The dictionary defines purpose as the reason for which something exists or is done. Purpose is a big deal and is important to your physical, mental, and emotional health. Knowing what your purpose is and operating in what you are called to do allows you to live a fulfilled life. Society may have conditioned you to believe that your life's purpose is to get married and have a family and earn a certain income. Finding your personal sense of purpose often brings much more fulfillment than being a wife, having children, or earning a certain amount of money.

Yes, there's purpose in those things, but I'm speaking of the greatest calling on your life. The purpose behind your life should motivate you to make a positive impact on the world, no matter how big or small it is.

Your purpose gives your life meaning, stability, and a sense of direction. It serves as the sustaining force that guides you day by day through the years. Your purpose is different from a goal. Goals can be achieved, but your purpose is never a completed task.

Wanting to be a mom is a goal that is achievable, but wanting to be a great mother is more of an intention than an achievement. Finding your purpose and operating in it is the key to living a happy and healthier life. Being happy and healthier can aid in living a longer life.

Even when you experience the storms of life, purpose serves as an anchor, providing stability and acting as your life compass. Sadly, a lot of people roam through life without a sense of purpose or direction. That's one of the worst things that can happen to someone. If you are needing support in this area, I encourage you to visit my website (keisacampbell.com) and book a consultation. Mark Twain said, "The two most important days in your life are the day you are born and the day you find out why."

So, what truly gives your life purpose? Is it solely the routine tasks of domestic life – coming home to prepare dinner, giving baths, checking homework, and attending dance recitals and tee ball games? While these responsibilities hold significance, you are missing the mark on what purpose truly is. Purpose extends beyond these daily duties. Yes, I know we have to feed the family, check the homework, and attend to all of the beautiful things that our children are in and there's purpose in those things, however, it's essential to recognize a broader purpose that fulfills your personal aspirations.

For me, guiding women towards self-discovery and empowerment which leads to Beautiful Living, is my life's purpose. The immerse fulfillment I experience from assisting them in discovering their true selves, being their co-pilot on their journey to purpose, and helping them launch their ventures is rewarding.

Before saying, "I do" and before becoming a mom, I believe there were desires and dreams in your whole heart yearning to be pursued. However, these aspirations may have taken a backseat to family obligations. Recognizing and pursuing these dreams can bring a deeper sense of fulfillment, complementing the responsibilities of family life.

I can resonate with that. When I was married, cooking, giving baths, checking homework, and attending cheer competitions, football games (because my daughters were cheerleaders), track meets, and dance recitals and competitions were my life. That's what came with the territory when having a family. In addition to those things, I would often call family meetings to discuss what it was that they wanted to do in that phase of their life. I heard cheer, I heard dance, and I knew it was my husband's deepest desire to become a full-time actor. My response to them all, DONE!

I would get so excited hearing the things that they wished to do that it moved me to act. When the girls said that they wanted to cheer, it happened. When the girls said that they wanted to dance, it happened. Cheer and dance became interchangeable for my daughters over years and throughout high school. My then-husband would go on auditions when he could because of work. He wasn't happy with his 9 to 5 and one day out of the blue, I said, "quit!" In astonishment, he said, "Are you serious?" I replied yes. I had not looked at the finances or anything, but I wanted them to live a fulfilled life. I wanted them to be happy and he resigned and pursued his acting career for a period of time.

I worked a full-time job at the local public school system and was in the hair salon part-time as a hairstylist. I sacrificed not being able to get my nails done, not being able to even buy myself a shirt, so that I could make sure that the girls did not feel a difference with only one income coming into the house. No one asked what it was that I wanted to do, I put myself on the back burner to help them live fulfilling lives. Although I felt like I had put myself on the back burner, I realized when I had those meetings, I was helping them to live out the vision for their lives which brought me fulfillment. I was wanting them to create their beautiful life. I would get excited hearing what they wanted to do and would go into action with a plan to make it happen. I wanted the girls to see that they could try anything that they wanted to in life and what they spoke came to pass. I was doing with them what I desired to do for women in the world but at that moment, I didn't realize it.

Your purpose is something that you have been doing all along, and you probably never sat still long enough to realize that it brings you fulfillment and that God wants you to use it to make an impact in the world. My purpose is to teach, encourage, inspire, and motivate women to live purposefully and embrace fulfilled lives beyond societal roles. It's about guiding them to rediscover their true selves. While the methods of how I do it may evolve, the essence of my purpose remains unchanged.

Reflecting on my journey, I realize that the seeds of my purpose were sown as early as 8 years old. It all began with a simple yet profound request from my cousin – to teach her how to plait her doll's hair. One evening, while playing with our baby doll, she observed me plaiting my doll's hair. Inspired by what she saw, she expressed a desire to learn herself.

Despite her being 12 years old, she boldly declared that we weren't going to bed until she learned…the nerve. I taught her in steps. I guided her through the process with patience, encouragement, and inspiration. Witnessing her determination and enthusiasm to achieve her goal, I didn't realize at that moment that I was already operating within a calling—a purpose that would later become clear to me.

I had another memorable experience that I recall during my high school years, this time involving a gym teacher. I vividly remember walking into the girls' locker room one day and noticing her sitting alone on a bench, with tears streaming down her face. Without hesitation, I approached her, feeling a mix of concern and empathy. I took a seat beside her and ask what was wrong. As she began to share, it became evident that she had received unfavorable news from her doctor. I listened intently, offering words of encouragement and support.

As I prepared to leave the room, I noticed a remarkable change in her demeanor. The tears that once flowed down her face had ceased, replaced by a subtle yet assuring nod of agreement. It was a small but significant shift, indicating that my words had resonated with her in some way. Before parting ways, she offered a heartfelt promise: that she would be present at my wedding when the time came. Years later, she fulfilled that promise, a touching reminder of the bond we had forged in that brief but impactful moment. I hugged her and left the locker room, unaware of the lasting impact my words would have on her. She later told me that I had changed her life with my words of encouragement.

Assisting others in bringing their visions to life brought me an immense sense of fulfillment, yet it took me some time to recognize that this act was deeply connected to my purpose. Holding frequent family meetings where I provided guidance and support to my loved ones as they pursued their dreams, became a natural part of my routine. However, it wasn't until later that I realized these gatherings were not just family obligations, but integral components of my purpose. It's a reminder that purpose isn't always grandiose or immediately apparent; sometimes, it's found in the seemingly ordinary moments of everyday life.

Your purpose is your why. The reason that you get out of bed in the morning, even when you are tired, and the day is gloomy. Even when the task that lies before you is hard or boring, you still get up to get it done because you are operating in purpose; you are moved to continue forward. It is essential not to compare your purpose to others; just as each fingerprint is unique, your purpose is as well. It's your calling, your destiny. Your purpose is related to your gifts and talents, your interest and experiences, and your skillsets that are all blended together and when used, you experience the greatest level of fulfillment.

When you wake up every day and you feel a sense of unfulfillment, experiencing misery, constantly feeling like you are on the hamster wheel of life, lacking joy and happiness, feeling out of place, and that your life looks exactly the same as it did the previous year but just with a different outfit, feeling like every day is the same ole thing, and you find yourself saying, "I know it has to be more to life than what I'm experiencing," it's highly possible that you are not operating in your purpose. Likely, you feel drained because you've had to be strong and take care of everyone else's needs. You dread going to your 9 to 5 and chances are, that's not what you are purposed to do. You have been ignoring moving on because you have told yourself that you need the money, which isn't enough anyway because you still find yourself living from paycheck to paycheck. Oh, and you need your health insurance, but do you not know that when you are doing what God has called you to do, He will supply all your needs (Philippians 4:19) and that He has already made provisions for your vision (Luke 9:10-17; 12:22-31)?

Living an unfulfilled life is not God's design for your life. God desires you to experience:

- Joy, happiness, and fulfillment

- Enhanced relationships and social life

- A long life

- Improved physical, mental, spiritual, and emotional health

- Increased optimism, resiliency, and hope

- More income

- A greater sense of belonging

Take a moment to reflect on these questions to help you recognize your purpose and how you can impact the world:

1. What activities or tasks consistently bring you fulfillment?

2. How can your interests and personal experiences be used to benefit others?

3. What unique gifts and talents do you possess, and how can you utilize them to make a meaningful impact in the world, whether on a large or small scale?

To live a fully satisfied life, you must have a sense of purpose. As a result, prioritization becomes easier, morals and values are strengthened, all your goals are aligned, and you stay focused. You can only achieve clarity in life if you have a clear sense of purpose.

P.S. I firmly believe that God has planted a business inside of every woman (yessss!), whether full-time or part-time, don't sit on it. Someone is waiting on what you have to offer.

EIGHT

Outward Beauty

"I praise you because I am fearfully and wonderfully made;

your works are wonderful, I know that full well."

Psalm 139:14 (NIV)

In the previous chapter, "Professional Beauty," the question was asked, "What is God calling you to do?" Once you identify that, you have to decide how you are going to show up for the calling. Outward Beauty is purposefully showing up for what God has called you to do. It's a celebration of the unique masterpiece that you are fearfully and wonderfully made for a purpose. So, why wouldn't you put your best foot forward when stepping out to make an impact in the world? This pillar of Beautiful Living was deliberately put last because I wanted to make sure that you addressed your mental, spiritual, physical, relational, and financial well-being, and had the opportunity to identify what your purpose might be.

Outward beauty is not just about physical appearance; it encompasses how you present yourself to the world, the confidence you exude, and the way you carry yourself. It reflects your commitment to fulfilling your purpose with excellence. When you recognize that you are fearfully and wonderfully made, you understand that God has uniquely crafted you for a specific purpose.

Often, we as women dress up our exterior and are a hot mess inwardly. Sometimes we show up flawless but haven't done the inward work. To be honest, it still shows up in your attitude and insecurities where we haven't done the internal work. As an image consultant, working with women, I get to see more than their outer beauty.

I remember styling a professional client and she told me what kind of things she liked, then she said, "I like how you dress, so like that." So, I went to work. When we had our fitting session, she began to tell me that she liked the things that I had chosen for her, but she didn't like her arms out, more specifically, she didn't like sleeveless tops, something that she didn't disclose to me in the beginning. I stood there in awe, thinking, "Why didn't you tell me this?" But I saw right through that, and I had to redirect the experience to a coaching session.

We got to the root of the issue and it had nothing to do with the clothes that I had selected for her. There were some internal things that had not been addressed until that moment. We worked through those things, and I styled her and baby when I tell you, she stepped out with a new level of confidence. Doing the inward work is essential, so when you step out into the world you are a better you and you are ready to make your mark in the world.

Once you have done the inner work, it's now time to get you all the way together from head to toe. Your appearance is often the first thing others notice about you. How you show up matters. Even when you are just going to the store, it matters. I'm not saying that you must be dressed to the nines at all time but what I am saying is that there should be a level of consideration in your attire. At no time should you be going out the door with a bonnet on your hair, in pajama pants, and house slippers. Those things were designed to be worn in the house. Additionally, just because something is in your size, it doesn't necessarily mean it complements your body type. It's essential to ensure that your hair is neat, your makeup is not overpowering (because you are already beautiful), and that you are dressed appropriately for the occasion. When you step out, it's not just about being cute; it's about being well-dressed and presenting yourself in a way that reflects self-respect and confidence.

Putting your best foot forward involves embracing your authentic self, acknowledging your strengths and weaknesses, and being intentional about your growth. It's about aligning your outward presentation with the inner qualities that make you a valuable and impactful individual. Your outward beauty is a reflection of the internal beauty that God has instilled within you.

I am one who has loved to dress nice my entire life. Over the years, I've asked people to tell me some things that they felt have never changed about me, and besides being an encourager and an inspirer, they said, "How you dress." I've heard, "Keisa you dress so nice," to "I mean how early do you have to get up to get dressed because you are always put together," to "I stand in my closet trying to think of something to wear and think, what would Keisa put together." I love the way I feel when I put on clothes. I love the way I look when I get dressed and I have a sense of joy when I leave out the door feeling well-dressed from my head to my feet.

Collins dictionary defines well-dress (adj) as attired in clothing that is of good quality, is properly fitted, and is appropriate and becoming. When you walk out your door and show up in the world, you are your own brand. It doesn't matter if you work a 9 to 5, if you are in ministry, or if you are a business owner. What matters is what you want your unique brand to be. What is your brand saying about you? When you step out, what message do you want to convey to the world? Is it that you are confident, you're a boss, you are ready to get some stuff done, you are fearfully and wonderfully made, and you represent the kingdom?

Feeling well-dressed creates a positive attitude. It boosts your self-confidence and the more confident you become, the more you can hear that little voice in your head say, "I can do this." When you are feeling good, you have a greater sense of motivation to get things done and feel accomplished. And when you feel good, your relationships benefit from it and there's a stronger sense of authentic self. In order to succeed in life, confidence is necessary, it helps you to feel more equipped to take on the world. Feeling confident and having self-respect convey that you are worth listening to and respecting. If you wish to move up in life, you must have confidence so why not put some clothes on it?

Here are some tips that you can follow to get started on your journey for showing up for who God has called you to be. Not just cute, but well-dressed.

1. *Determine who you want to be.* Do the inner work so that when you show up, you are beautiful from the inside out. Then you can show up as the beautiful person you envision yourself to be.

2. *Declutter your closet.* Get rid of all the things that you no longer wear to make space for pieces that truly align with your style and identity. Removing unused items streamlines your wardrobe, making it more functional. This step promotes a clutter-free environment, allowing you to focus on pieces you genuinely love. There's no purpose in having things that you are not using take up space.

3. *Find your personal style.* Finding your personal style is an exploratory journey. I recommend crafting an inspiration board or mood board, a valuable tool aiding you in visualizing your envisioned personal style using images, material samples, and color palettes. This process assists in defining and refining your preferences, fostering intentional choices when shopping and selecting outfits.

4. *Learn how to balance your body proportions.* Discovering how to dress for your specific body shape enables you to identify the clothing that complements

your figure and those that don't. This knowledge empowers you to avoid wasting time on clothes that won't enhance your appearance and instead focus on selecting garments that are tailored to your body shape. For detailed guidance on dressing for your body type, grab my eBook "Release the Style Within You" available at keisacampbell.com/shop.

5. *Experiment with color.* I love experimenting with color, it's fun, and the possibilities are limitless. If you are hesitant of incorporating color into your wardrobe, start with a single colorful piece until you are more comfortable, then gradually introduce additional colors. This gradual approach allows you to explore and express your personal style in a way that feels comfortable and authentic.

6. *Have reliable wardrobe staples.* Your reliable staples are a great-fitting suit in dark or lighter neutrals, the iconic little black dress (every woman needs one), a nice pair of jeans that fit you perfectly, simple T-shirts, white or

neutral-colored button-downs, and a leather or denim jacket. Having these reliable wardrobe staples ensures that you're well -prepared for a variety of occasions, offering flexibility and ease in creating diverse outfits that align with your personal style.

Consider every aspect of your life as an opportunity to demonstrate your outward beauty – from your interactions with others to the way you pursue your goals. Showcasing your God-given gifts and talents is an act of gratitude for the marvelous creation that you are. As you step into the world with purpose, remember that your outward beauty is a testament to the incredible workmanship of God.

So, you must decide what type of woman you want to be and show up for her. The next time that you leave the house, ask yourself: Are you showing up as the woman you envision yourself to be and are you are representing what God has called you to do? Am I conveying what my brand is? Remember, you are a brand no matter if you work a 9 to 5. This is not exclusive to just business owners. You must show up every time you leave the house because you never know whom you are destined to meet. You need to be ready. So, put your best foot forward, confidently embracing the beauty within you, and let it shine for the world to see.

BONUS

Social Beauty

"And let us consider how we may spur one another on toward love and good deeds, not giving up meeting together, as some are in the habit of doing, but encouraging one another—and all the more as you see the Day approaching."

Hebrews 10:24-25 (NIV)

As I was bringing this book to closure, I thought to myself about the importance of being social and how it goes hand in hand with "Relational Beauty." Have you ever noticed that life becomes a little brighter when you're surrounded by friends and people who care about you? Well, that's what social beauty is all about. It's like the magic that happens when you step out of your comfort zone and connect with others. Picture a world where we're not meant to walk alone but to journey together, hand in hand, heart to heart. That's the essence of social beauty, and it's a vital part of the human experience. I thought I would share more about its benefits and why you should apply it to your life.

I've always believed that God designed us for community. God didn't create us to be loners; instead, He wired us to be social beings. Just like pieces of a puzzle fit together to create a beautiful picture, we, too, fit into a community to create a beautiful life. It's about sharing laughter, wiping away tears, and creating memories with others. There's something special about forming connections with others, a joy that happens when hearts come together in friendship and camaraderie.

Reflecting on my own life, I can't remember a time when I didn't have friends around when needed. As I expressed in chapter five, "Relational Beauty," cultivating relationships are important to me. One thing that I've noticed is that when women get married or in new relationships, they sometimes unintentionally drift away from the friendships that they have cultivated. This might happen because of busy schedules or the belief that marriage should be the sole focus or perhaps due to the excitement of a new romantic relationship. However, neglecting friendships can result in feeling isolated, relying too much on one's spouse for emotional support, and missing out on personal development opportunities. There needs to be a healthy balance.

When I was married, nurturing my friendships were essential for maintaining balance in my life. Those moments of laughter and shared experiences were like beacons of light, guiding me through the darkest times in my life.

Even when life threw me curveballs, my friendships stood as pillars of strength. And when my marriage faced challenges, getting out to socialize became crucial. It wasn't just about having fun; it was what I needed to helped me redirect my energy and find joy amid difficult times.

And then came the storm of my divorce. In those tough times, forming new connections and embracing social opportunities became not just a choice but a lifeline. It was in the laughter of newfound friends and the warmth of community gatherings that I found the strength to pick up the pieces of my shattered heart and start over. Socializing became my refuge, a sanctuary where I could rediscover myself and find joy amidst the chaos.

In a world that often inundates women with many roles and expectations, finding time to be social can seem like a daunting task. But amidst the hustle and bustle of daily life, it's crucial to carve out moments for connection and camaraderie. Here are six simple yet profound ways for you to cultivate social beauty in their lives:

1. *Girls' night out.* Plan regular outings with your closest girlfriends. Whether it's dinner at a cozy restaurant, a movie night at home, or a fun-filled day of shopping, spending quality time with friends can rejuvenate the soul. As Ecclesiastes 4:9-10 reminds us, "Two are better than one, because they have a good return on their labor: If either of them falls down, one can help the other up. But pity anyone who falls and has no one to help them up!"

2. *Join a club or group.* Explore your interests and hobbies by joining clubs or groups in your community. Whether

it's a book club, a yoga class, or a volunteer organization, participating in activities you enjoy can help you meet like-minded women and form meaningful connections.

3. *Attend social events.* Keep an eye out for social events happening in your area, such as parties, festivals, or community gatherings. This can be two-fold. If you have a business, it can be a way to meet new people in your industry for possible collaborations and also can lead to unexpected friendships. Stepping out of your comfort zone and mingling with new people can lead to enriching experiences.

4. *Volunteer.* Dedicate some of your time to volunteer work for a cause you're passionate about. Not only will you be making a positive impact in your community, but you'll also have the opportunity to meet people who share your values and interests.

5. *Take classes or workshops.* Enroll in classes or workshops that pique your curiosity, whether it's

cooking, painting, or learning a new language. Not only will you gain new skills, but you'll also have the chance to connect with others who share your enthusiasm for learning and growth.

6. *Host gatherings.* Don't wait for social opportunities to come to you—create them! Host gatherings or parties at your home and invite friends, family, and neighbors to come together for food, fun, and fellowship. Opening your doors to others can cultivate a sense of warmth and hospitality that strengthens bonds and fosters community.

In a world that often pulls us in a million different directions, it's essential to prioritize social beauty and the connections that nourish our souls. As Proverbs 27:17 reminds us, "As iron sharpens iron, so one person sharpens another." By investing in relationships and embracing the beauty of social interaction, we not only enrich our own lives but also uplift and inspire those around us. So let's journey together, hand in hand, as we embrace the beauty of community and the joy of shared moments.

BEAUTIFUL LIVING SUMMARY

What is Beautiful Living?

Beautiful Living is living and operating in your purpose. It's cultivating a healthy mindset, having an intimate relationship with God, taking care of the one temple that God has given you, maintaining a healthy relationship with yourself first and then with others. It's not living beyond your means, but it is serving others and making an impact in the world and it's showing up for who God has called you to be. Beautiful Living is finding harmony in your life and releasing those things and people who no longer serve you. It's whole-life wellness.

It is God's desire for you to know why He created you and for you to live a fulfilled life. Whether you are a mom or a wife, there is Beautiful Living that awaits you beyond your roles. Even if you are a divorcee, know that all hope is not lost and that there is

Beautiful Living after divorce. For all, you are the only one who can define what Beautiful Living looks like for you. It will look different for everyone. Fulfillment is based on your values, your beliefs, and your deepest needs.

While achieving goals throughout life is a precursor to fulfillment, it isn't the whole story. True happiness is found in living and operating in your purpose, which God has called you to. So, I can't define it for you, but I can come along on the journey with you as your co-pilot. Yes, there will be some curve balls thrown your way from time to time, but it doesn't mean that you allow them to stifle you from moving forward. I know you want more; I know that you are tired of being on the merry-go-round of life. Whatever you envision for your life can be attained but it starts with you saying yes to YOU.

When I was approached with an opportunity to run for Ms. Georgia, my initial thought was, "Girl no. I'm not about to be in nobody's pageant." I just finished reading Shonda Rhimes, "A Year of Yes." I reflected on how much I gave of myself to others and at that moment, I decided that I was going to go for it. The day that I found out that I won was the same day my divorce was final. Right then, doors were opening for me to start my new journey to Beautiful Living. It's time to take a chance on you. It's time to say yes to you. Beautiful Living is your birthright, and it is available to you. You just have to claim it for yourself and do the work. I believe in you! To experience Beautiful Living is truly a joy. So, what will your story be? Let's start the journey!

Know that…

Beautiful Living Awaits You!

ACKNOWLEDGEMENTS

First and foremost, I want to thank God for entrusting me with this transformative assignment. This journey has been nothing short of a divine assignment, and I am humbled by the guidance and inspiration received throughout the writing process. Thank you for choosing me for this purpose; I am truly honored to be an instrument of your message.

To my beautiful daughters, TaBresha, Teryn, and Kennedy, you are the radiant stars that brighten my sky and the endless source of my inspiration. Thank you for teaching me the profound meaning of motherhood and for instilling in me the desire to continuously evolve. May your lives be graced with fulfillment, and may you always have the courage to pursue your dreams with unwavering determination. Know that your light is unlimited, and may it forever illuminate the world around you. I will always have your back and I love you all deeply.

ACKNOWLEDGEMENT

To my sisters, your unwavering love and support have been a constant source of strength. A special expression of gratitude to my sister Tuwanna; you have consistently shown up for me. I appreciate you more than words can convey, thank you. To my sister Alicia, thank you for your lending ear and for being the big little sister when needed and to my sister Chantrice, well you already know how we get down. Much love to all of my sisters.

To my parents, Alvin and Virginia, thank you for giving birth to me and instilling in me the values that have guided me on my path. I love you.

I extend my gratitude to everyone who has supported me along the way. Your encouragement, kindness, and belief in my message have been invaluable. Your love fuels my passion for spreading the message of Beautiful Living.

In closing, I want to express my deep love and appreciation to each person who has been a part of this incredible journey. Your presence, support, and love have been the driving force behind the realization of this dream. I am forever grateful, and I love you all.

NOTES

1. https://blog.psecu.com/learn/financial-tips-for-every-stage-in-life/2020/09/24/how-to-foster-a-positive-money-mindset

2. https://wellnesscenter.uic.edu/news-stories/boundaries-what-are-they-and-how-to-create-them/#:~:text=Setting%20boundaries%20is%20a%20form,we%20feel%20respected%20and%20safe

3. https://scopeblog.stanford.edu/2019/08/02/the-benefits-of-self-forgiveness/

4. https://www.linkedin.com/pulse/three-reasons-people-come-our-life-denise-forney/

ABOUT THE AUTHOR

Mom at 14, married at 21, and divorced by 40, **KEISA CAMPBELL** is the epitome of resilience, femininity, and women empowerment. Teenage motherhood, birthing three daughters, and coaching girlfriends (since elementary) are what cultivated her maternal insight, journey to purpose, and passion for serving women. Keisa learned very early that giving up was not an option and that trials were only indicators of how bright her future would be.

Crowned Ms. Georgia 2019 in the Mr. & Mrs. Black America Pageant, she is a multi-talented speaker, certified professional life and beauty coach, and author. Keisa is the founder and CEO of Beautiful Living, a holistic wellness brand created to impact, inspire, and help women live more significantly. Founded on seven pillars, Beautiful Living focuses on mental, spiritual, physical, relational, financial, career, and outward beauty. Through her brand, Keisa partners with women from all backgrounds to cultivate a healthy mindset and vision while defining purpose and strategies to live beautifully.

> *"Transformation starts in the mind, and living beautifully means transforming disempowering circumstances into positive life experiences."*
>
> *-Keisa Campbell, Founder and CEO of Beautiful Living.*

She has a Bachelor's in Business Administration and over 20 years of experience transforming women's lives. Featured in VoyageATL, Shoutout Atlanta, and BOLD Journey, Keisa is the author of Release the Style Within You and Recalculating Route. Learn more about Keisa and Beautiful Living at www.keisacampbell.com

Access exclusive bonus content and resources to deepen your journey to Beautiful Living as a complimentary gift. Scan QR code.

Milton Keynes UK
Ingram Content Group UK Ltd.
UKHW010639040324
438885UK00001B/146